Walther Ziegler

AF199201

Hobbes
in 60 Minutes

Translated by
Alexander Reynolds

My thanks go to Rudolf Aichner for his tireless critical editing; Silke Ruthenberg for the fine graphics; Lydia Pointvogl, Eva Amberger, Christiane Hüttner, and Dr. Martin Engler for their excellent work as manuscript readers and sub-editors; Prof. Guntram Knapp, who first inspired me with enthusiasm for philosophy; and Angela Schumitz, who handled in the most professional manner, as chief editorial reader, the production of both the German and the English editions of this series of books.

My special thanks go to my translator

Dr Alexander Reynolds.

Himself a philosopher, he not only translated the original German text into English with great care and precision but also, in passages where this was required in order to ensure clear understanding, supplemented this text with certain formulations adapted specifically to the needs of English-language readers.

Bibliographic Information held by the German National Library: The details of the original German edition of this publication are held by the German National Library as part of the German National Bibliography; detailed bibliographical data can be found online at www.dnb.de.

1st Edition July 2020
Jacket design and graphic design for the whole book: Silke Ruthenberg, making use of illustrations by:
Raphael Bräsecke, Creactive – Studio for Advertising, Comics & Illustrations
© JackF - Fotolia.com (image-frames)
© Valerie Potapova - Fotolia.com (image-frames)
© Svetlana Gryankina - Fotolia.com (speech-balloons)

Publisher and Printing:
BoD – Books on Demand, Norderstedt
ISBN 978-3-7519-6831-7

Contents

Hobbes's Great Discovery

Thomas Hobbes (1588-1679) is considered to be the founder of political philosophy. He is certainly one of the most significant thinkers of the early Modern Age. His theory of the state remains, still today, a basic building-block of our modern self-understanding and we still hear cited, everywhere in the world, his famous claim that "Man is a wolf to Man" or, to cite Hobbes more precisely

Man to Man is an arrant wolf.[2]

Although Hobbes wrote this sentence in 1651, that is, almost 400 years ago, it is still very well known. Already in his own lifetime this, Hobbes's deeply pessimistic view of human nature attracted much attention, often negative. It provoked, in particular, a bitter critique from the church. Thus, all his writings came to be banned as heretical.

This is hardly surprising, since Hobbes was one of the first characteristically "modern" thinkers and took a position radically opposed to the traditional notions of Paradise, Adam and Eve, and the Creation of Man in God's image. Hobbes was a convinced atheist and an adherent to the principles of the new natural sciences just then on the rise. The universe, Hobbes argued, is, scientifically considered, in no sense the expression of some brilliant divine mind but rather, initially at least, no more than just an accumulation of physical bodies:

[...] The universe, that is, the whole mass of things that are, is corporeal [...] and hath the dimensions of magnitude, namely, length, breadth and depth.[3]

From this Hobbes draws a radical conclusion:

And because the universe is all that which is, no part of it is *nothing*, and consequently *nowhere*.[4]

It follows from this that God, who certainly does not form any "corporeal" part of the physical universe that one might measure in terms of "length, breadth and depth", must likewise be "nothing and nowhere". When asked how he conceived of God, Hobbes used to reply that no human being, not even a theologian, could possibly form a notion of Him or of His qualities. For this reason, he went on, it was high time that the attempt be made to explain the world, the state and the purpose of human life in purely scientific terms, without any reference to God. By reasoning in this way Hobbes contradicted the medieval idea of a "divine right" to rulership and laid the foundations for his own project of providing humanity, for the very first time, with a purely logically comprehensible theory of the best possible mode of co-existence within the state. The most important precondition of this theory was a clear recognition of human beings' basic nature. It was necessary to understand, he argued

[...] What the quality of human nature is (and) in what matters it is, (and) in what matters it is not, fit to make up a civil government [...]⁵

And the epoch-making result at which Hobbes arrived was that human nature was, in the final analysis, such that human beings were not fit to come together and form a state or a polity. Man's wolf-like nature, so Hobbes argued, tended to problematize and prevent people's natural co-existence and even, in the end, made this natural co-existence quite impossible. But how exactly did Hobbes arrive at this pessimistic conclusion?

Hobbes was a child prodigy. Already at age four he could read and write and retained these skills also into an age that, for many, is a "second infancy": he produced an English translation of Homer when he was almost ninety. He studied in Oxford, where he acquired several languages, became private secretary to Sir Francis Bacon and got to know, on the journeys on which he accompanied this latter, such great contemporaries as Descartes and Galileo. He was especially fascinated by Galileo and by the latter's theory, revolutionary at the time, whereby all physical bodies, including the planets, are in constant motion.

Galileo's notion helped Hobbes to develop his own key idea. If Galileo was right and all physical bodies were in constant motion, with even the planets following specific orbital courses and obeying physical laws, then human beings too, being physical bodies in their turn, had necessarily to comply with certain drives and laws of motion. And it was indeed with "motion" that Hobbes began his investigation and explanation of all human life and activity:

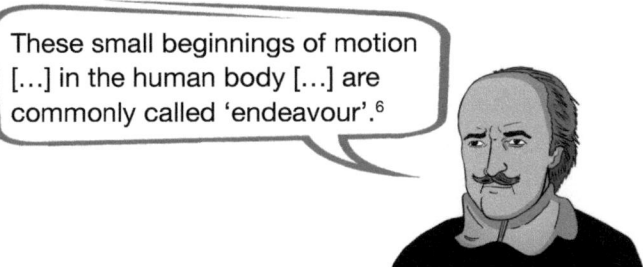

These small beginnings of motion [...] in the human body [...] are commonly called 'endeavour'.[6]

"Endeavour", Hobbes goes on to say, can either be "endeavour toward" something, in which case we speak of "desire", or "endeavour away" from it, in which case we speak of "aversion":

That which men desire they are also said to love, and to hate those things for which they have aversion.[7]

In Hobbes's view our human lives consist, considered purely scientifically, in nothing but these two motions: the motion of our bodies toward something or away from something. That which we love, desire or wish for we seek out; that which we hate, fear or abhor we avoid. But both these types of movement are aimed, in the last analysis, at one and the same goal:

> The greatest of goods for each is his own preservation. For Nature is so arranged that all desire good for themselves.[8]

Human beings, argued Hobbes, naturally wish to go on living and pursue, therefore, their own, as he calls it, "good". And since they wish to secure this "good" not just for the present moment but also for the future and ideally for their whole life, they also, necessarily, desire power. They require this power in order to be sure of their self-preservation: for example, in order to defend their hunting ground, their harvest or their home:

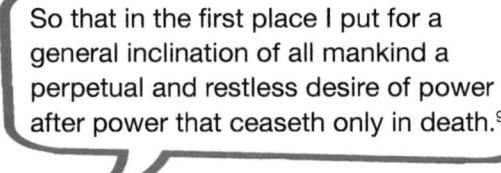

> So that in the first place I put for a general inclination of all mankind a perpetual and restless desire of power after power that ceaseth only in death.[9]

This drive toward power inherent in the very nature of Man is, for Hobbes, nothing morally reprehensible but does indeed, just like the will to survive, belong to the fundamental traits with which Nature has equipped the human species. Human beings, Hobbes believes, simply cannot do otherwise than constantly seek to increase their personal power:

[...] The cause of this [...] is that he cannot assure the power and means to live well, which he hath present(ly), without the acquisition of more (power).[10]

If there were no laws, rules or regulations, argues Hobbes, human beings would give free rein to their inborn nature and would try constantly to extend their power so as to secure their personal survival. There would arise a violent competitive struggle over scarce commodities. This condition without laws or regulations Hobbes calls "the state of Nature". Certain Native Americans, Hobbes believed, were still in his day living in such a lawless state, without any form of police or legal system. Their tribes carried out attacks one on the other and found themselves in possession, depending on the outcomes of these attacks, at times of more land and horses, at times of less. But civilized peoples too, Hobbes argued, tend to fall back into this "state of Nature" as soon as the state is no longer able to ensure social order:

I demonstrate in the first place that the state of men without civil society (which state we may properly call the state of

Nature) is nothing else but a mere war of all against all and in that war all men have equal right unto all things.[11]

Since in the "state of Nature" there are no laws or regulations each man has a natural right to all he desires. But just these two factors, the natural will to survive and its attendant will to power along with the "equal right to all things", make of this "state of Nature" a state of endless, dangerous struggle and conflict:

If now [...] you add the right of all to all, whereby one by right invades, the other by right resists, [...] it cannot be denied but that the natural state of men,

before they entered into society, was a mere war, and that not simply, but a war of all men against all men.[12]

This claim of Hobbes to the effect that the "state of Nature", lacking all state-set laws, must inevitably sink into a "war of all against all" is a claim that, even centuries later, continues to provoke and excite debate. Hobbes's core idea is that human beings are by their very nature creatures unsuited to living peacefully in society with one another. Such a living peacefully together is made possible only by the artful establishment of a state with laws, policemen and judges. Hobbes stresses the "artful", meaning "artificial", nature of the measures by which human beings can alone be brought to live in peace:

For by art is created that great *Leviathan*, *called a commonwealth, or state* [...][13]

The securing of internal and external peace, then, is, for Hobbes, the most important task and, indeed, the sole justification for the existence of this "state or commonwealth". Such a state must be strong enough to keep in check all the individuals and groups that make it up. This is why Hobbes calls it also "the great Leviathan", alluding to the Biblical monster of this name which is described in the Old Testament as stronger and more fearsome than any other creature on earth.

Hobbes's central idea, then, is both provocative and revolutionary. It is not on any impulse or instinct natural to human beings that we can rely in order to ensure our social co-existence; on the contrary, social co-existence is ensured only through the suppression of these natural impulses and instincts by the state. Is Hobbes right here? Are we perhaps really, considered in terms of our essential human nature, not the sociable, altruistic beings in need of the love of our fellow man that we like to believe we are but rather power-hungry egoists skilled above all at ensuring our own survival?

Are we really protected only by a thin veneer of civilization from our own essentially wolf-like nature and from a bloody war of all against all? And if so, of what use can it be to us to understand this? There can be no doubt: Hobbes remains a challenging and provocative thinker even almost four centuries on.

Hobbes's Central Idea

"Homo Homini Lupus" –
The Wolf-Like Nature of Man

Homo homini lupus is a phrase which can be translated "Man is a wolf to Man". Nowadays, it is a phrase inextricably associated in people's minds with Hobbes. It was, however, not originally his own. He drew a similar phrase from the much less well-known ancient Roman author Titus Maccius Plautus and remodelled it for the purposes of his own theory.[14]

At first glance one might understand the phrase to mean that one must always be on one's guard against one's fellow human beings because these latter are always, in their inmost hearts, predators, hungry and morally unscrupulous competitors for everything. In short, the message would be: Man is wicked. But this is only part of the truth about Hobbes's intention in using the phrase. Hobbes was concerned above all to show how human beings would behave in a situation ungoverned by any law, a situation in which there was no state, no civilization and thus no regulation laying down social rules for what is "good" and what is "evil".

What counts above all else in such a lawless, anarchistic, primitive society is ensuring one's bare survival. Man may not be essentially wicked but he has no choice except to do all that is in his power to do when it comes to ensuring his own survival. This instinct of self-preservation is natural and unproblematic so long as each individual is simply seeking his personal nourishment and consuming it on the spot. Problems arise, however, where two individuals or groups both covet the same object. For example, where both lay claim to the same bountiful valley, the same field to grow crops on, or the same hunting ground. Conflict may also arise where someone is inhabiting a wind-sheltered cave that another person may wish for himself:

> And therefore if any two men desire the same thing, which nevertheless they cannot both enjoy, they become enemies.[15]

It is in such situations that "Man becomes a wolf to Man" – but not because Man is essentially morally corrupt, let alone wicked. His instinct of self-preservation, and the actions that this necessitates, compel him to do what he does:

The notions of right and wrong, justice and injustice, have there no place.[16]

In the "state of Nature" Man simply does that which his nature dictates to him, even if we are loth to accept what this is:

It may seem strange to some man that has not weighed well these things […] that Nature should […] render men apt to invade and destroy one another.[17]

But experience teaches us, says Hobbes, that such is indeed the case. Nature, indeed, cannot be blamed for this. We cannot reproach Nature with being what it is:

[...] But neither of us accuse Man's nature in it. The desires and other passions of Man are no sin in themselves. No more are the actions that proceed from those passions till they know a law that forbids them.[18]

As gravity or centrifugal force for the planets, the drive to self-preservation is, for Man, the basic force that keeps us, our whole life long, in constant movement. This applies, indeed, not just to "the state of Nature". We "civilized human beings" also strive to survive. We consult doctors if we are ill, buy warm clothes for the winter; see to it that we earn money; attempt to live as comfortably and in as good health as possible; and secure our houses against burglary and theft. But in the "civilized" condition of a society governed by a state human beings' will to self-preservation plays out within the framework of fixed rules and laws regulating property and exchange of property. In the "state of Nature", by contrast, there are no supermarkets, property leases, or regular monetary incomes. The needs of different human beings crash and collide with one another in a completely unregulated and uninhibited way:

> And therefore if any two men desire the same thing [...] in the way to their end [...] which is principally their own conservation [...] (they) endeavour to destroy or subdue one another.[19]

But competition for scarce goods is not the only reason why, in the "state of Nature", each man must become "a wolf" to other men:

> [...] In the nature of Man we find three principal causes of quarrel. First, competition; secondly, diffidence; thirdly, glory.[20]

Hobbes uses the word "diffidence" here in its 17th-century rather than its modern sense, referring rather to something that we would call, today, "mistrust".

The problem of mistrust is the problem that human beings, being naturally equipped with reason, will equally naturally always try to gain a strategic advantage. This is a tendency which we must assume to exist not only in ourselves but in everyone that we encounter. We need always to be fundamentally mistrustful because we compete, in the "state of Nature", not only for things that we need to survive at each present moment, i.e. for things to quench our immediate hunger and thirst, but also for what is required to ensure that our future needs will also be met. This being the case, human beings can be more merciless than any beast of prey:

Man surpasseth in rapacity and cruelty the wolves, bears and snakes, (being) famished even by future hunger.[21]

Other animals are satisfied and settle down to sleep once they have eaten and drunk their fill. Man, however, remains constantly tense and on the alert:

The cause whereof is that the object of Man's desire is not to enjoy once only [...] but to assure forever the way of his future desire. And therefore the [...]

the [...] inclinations of all men tend not only to the procuring but also to the assuring of a contented life.[22]

Such an "assuring of a contented life" not just at present but in future requires, then, the personal power to keep all one's enemies in check and even to dominate them:

By consequence, such augmentation of dominion over men being necessary to a man's conservation, it ought to be allowed him.[23]

Hobbes also mentions as a "cause of quarrel" competition and the attempt to increase power that comes along with it. And finally, as a third "cause of quarrel"

in the "state of Nature", he speaks of the desire for "glory", that is to say, the struggle to be respected and honoured by other human beings. This, among the three causes named by Hobbes, is the only one that is not related to the imperatives of simple physical survival. Hobbes mentions it, nonetheless, because it is an impulse deeply rooted in human nature. Nietzsche too later noted vanity of this sort to be a vice so deeply rooted in humanity that there would likely never be found any remedy for it. Thus, it is possible that a violent quarrel over "glory" might arise from

[…] trifles, such as a word, a smile, a different opinion, and any other sign of undervalue […][24]

But besides these three "causes of quarrel" in Hobbes's "state of Nature", namely, "competition", "diffidence" and "glory", there is also a more comprehensive structural reason why Man here "becomes a wolf to Man". This is the natural equality that tends to exist between human beings as regards our bodily strength and intellectual capacity. Since all human beings possess in these regards more or less the same level of ability, all will tend to perceive there to be at least a chance of their getting what they need by force or cunning. Hobbes is aware, indeed, that certain disparities in size and physique do exist between one human being and another. But he is of the view that such small disparities play in the end, in the "state of Nature", no role that is really worth mentioning:

For as to the strength of body, the weakest has strength enough to kill the strongest, either by secret machination, or by confederacy with others [...][25]

There exists, indeed, Hobbes claims, an even greater degree of equality between human beings regarding mental capacities than there does regarding physical ones. Some may possess a little more wit and fluency than others but in the last analysis human intellect is more or less evenly distributed. Hobbes cites in support of this claim one particularly original piece of evidence. No one has ever been heard, says Hobbes, to complain that he has been equipped by Nature with too little intellect:

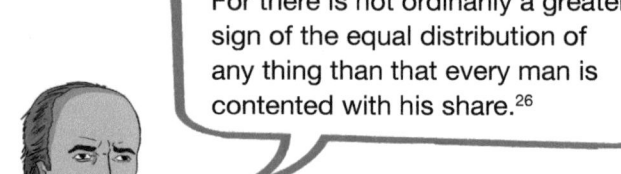

For there is not ordinarily a greater sign of the equal distribution of any thing than that every man is contented with his share.[26]

This equal distribution of corporeal and mental capacities sounds at first as though it is an entirely good and positive thing. It tends, however, to provide, in the "state of Nature", yet another cause of struggle and conflict:

From this equality of ability ariseth equality of hope in the attaining of our ends.[27]

The "War of All Against All" in the State of Nature

There must then, argues Hobbes, inevitably arise a "war of all against all". It proves no more possible to remove from life in the "state of Nature" a violent competition for food and for safe places to sleep and live than it does to remove the actions needed to protect against present and future attacks by other human beings. And such inborn human traits as the urge to constantly extend one's power and to acquire renown and respect among one's fellows see to it that we do not find peace even when we have made tolerably sure of our short-term and longer-term physical survival:

Hereby it is manifest that, during the time that men live without a common power to keep them all in awe, they

are in that condition that is called 'war', and such a war as is of every man against every man.[28]

27

Even if someone, in this "state of Nature", should have the great luck to acquire, be it by sheer physical force or by cunning, a sheltered cave or a well-defended fortress enclosing a cultivable field, he will be able to enjoy these things only for a short while:

> And from hence it comes to pass that [...] if one plant, sow, build or possess a convenient seat,

> others may probably be expected to come with forces united to dispossess and deprive him not only of the fruit of his labour but also of his life or liberty.[29]

There is, then, no way out of the state of war so long as there are no judges, police officers and prisons to set limits to human beings' living out of their natural needs and passions:

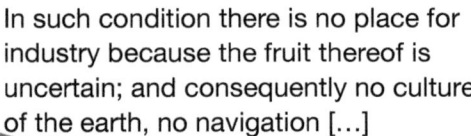

> In such condition there is no place for industry because the fruit thereof is uncertain; and consequently no culture of the earth, no navigation [...]

no arts, no letters [...] and, which is worst of all, continual fear and danger of violent death [...].[30]

It is at this point in the text of his *Leviathan* that Hobbes arrives at his pithiest and most famous conclusion regarding human existence in the "state of Nature":

And the life of Man (in this state of Nature is) solitary, poor, nasty, brutish and short.[31]

Already Hobbes's own contemporaries objected to Hobbes that he had drawn, with his talk of a "wolf-like human nature", a "war of all against all" and a "short, brutish life" marked by constant assaults and defences from assault, a far too negative picture of the human condition. Man after all, so these contemporaries of Hobbes pointed out, is also a social being. A far more positive image of human nature, for example, is to be found in the philosophy of antiquity. Aristotle, famously, had proposed that *Anthropos zoon politikon physei estin*: "Man is by his nature a political animal", that is to say, "an animal apt to live together in city-states".[32]

If one subscribes to this way of seeing things, Man has not a wolfish but rather a social nature and tends naturally to blossom and develop in community with other human beings. Human beings, according to the Aristotelian view, have always lived together in groups and are, just like animals that like to live in herds, by nature peaceful "species-beings".

Hobbes, however, directly and vigorously contradicts Aristotle on this point. It may well be that such creatures as bees and ants are of a nature such as to naturally form societies; but this, Hobbes insists, is not at all the case for Man:

It is true that certain living creatures, (such) as bees and ants, live sociably one with another […]

Amongst these creatures the common good differeth not from the private [...] But Man, whose joy consisteth in comparing himself with other men, can relish nothing but what is eminent.[33]

Whereas, then, bees and ants share all their goods with one another and ascribe no worth at all to their private, individual wellbeing, for example to a personal hoard of honey, it is the desire of Man always to distinguish himself from his fellows by some special clothing, habitation or other commodity. The reason for this, argues Hobbes, in the traits with which Nature itself has equipped Man, above all in the faculty of speech:

(Although) these creatures (bees and ants) [...] have some use of voice in making known to one another their desires [...] yet they want that

art of words by which some men can represent to others that which is good in the likeness of evil and evil in the likeness of good.[34]

Language, then, is, when used by human beings, in contrast to its rudimentary use by other animals, an extremely dangerous instrument. Human beings can use language to flatter, insult, lie, put rumours into circulation, and each to wound the vanity of the other. Besides language, the other problematical difference between Man and other animals is the former's possession of reason. Whereas human beings, being endowed with reason, are always worrying about their futures, other animals are capable of living in an eternal present moment:

And therefore, as long as they be at ease, they are not offended with their fellow, whereas Man is then most troublesome when he is most at ease.[35]

In view of these and several other differences from Man Hobbes arrives at the following conclusion regarding the co-existence of non-human animals:

The agreement of these creatures is natural; that of Man is by covenant only, which is artificial.[36]

It is here that Hobbes formulates for the first time, clearly and succinctly, his highly provocative central idea. Whereas, in a state composed of bees, peaceful coexistence is directly a work of Nature itself, for human beings to achieve such a condition a certain artfulness is needed. And this artfulness is the political state itself which serves to protect human individuals one from the other:

For by art is created that great *Leviathan*, called a commonwealth, or state [...][37]

Whereas, then, other animals can simply rely on their innate nature, Man must rather be on the alert before his. Because, as Hobbes argues, in the case of us human beings it is not our primary drives and instincts but rather, on the contrary, the taming, suppression and inhibition of these primary drives and instincts that ensures our survival.

The Natural "Right to Everything" and Why We Must Give It Up

In the "state of Nature" Man is still completely free and enjoys an unlimited natural right to all those things which seem in any way attractive to him:

Nature hath given to everyone a right to all. That is, it was lawful for every man in the bare state of Nature [...] to do what he would [...] and enjoy all he would, or could get.[38]

But this enormous freedom consisting in being able to freely pursue all one's needs has the equally great drawback that it must necessarily lead to the "war of all against all". The price paid for it, then, is a very high one. For this reason, there exists already in the "state of Nature" a number of so-called "natural laws" which urge us in the direction of keeping the peace and not constantly chafing and clashing against one another. One of these "natural laws", which have all the appearance of simple common sense, runs:

Seek peace, and follow it.[39]

This law can in fact be a very sensible one. It is one which suggests itself particularly strongly to human beings in the "state of Nature" since they get to feel, every day, how strenuous it is to live in a permanent state of war. A second "natural law" runs:

Quod tibi fieri non vis, alteri ne feceris (never do to others what you would not have done to yourself).[40]

This "natural law" too is one which suggests itself as basic common sense to us, since applying it would surely promote a better life for all, provided only that all abided by it. Were no one, indeed, any longer to inflict on anyone else things that he would not wish to have to suffer himself, such as being tortured, robbed or burgled, then we surely would all lead a more pleasant life. Already in the "state of Nature", then, human beings possess certain initial natural ideas regarding how they might more pleasantly and fruitfully live together. The great problem lies only in the fact that these "natural laws" are not really binding regulations with which all are obliged or compelled to comply:

These dictates of reason men used to call by the name of laws; but improperly, for they are but conclusions, or theorems [...][41]

When it comes down to it, these conclusions or theorems have no binding force. For them to have force, Hobbes insists, there needs to be a coercive power consisting of policemen and of judges who will positively see to it that the laws are observed:

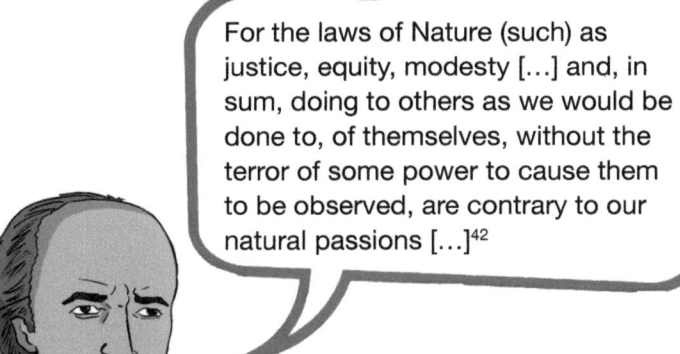

For the laws of Nature (such) as justice, equity, modesty [...] and, in sum, doing to others as we would be done to, of themselves, without the terror of some power to cause them to be observed, are contrary to our natural passions [...][42]

To sum up, then: the "natural right to everything" and to the living-out of all our passions and desires means, indeed, a total and unconditional freedom for the individual. But this absolute freedom is bought only at the price of a constant fear of death and is, therefore, experienced as something extremely threatening. For this reason even while they are still in the "state of Nature" human beings begin to form notions of laws and rules that might limit the war and struggle ensuing from their freedom. But it is indeed a matter here only of notions, that is to say, of mere words:

(They are) but words, and of no strength to secure a man at all.[43]

There can be no true security until, out of words, there emerge laws. And it is just this that happens with the establishment of a state.

The Social Contract –
The Birth of the Great Leviathan

The true act of establishing a state, which involves forgoing absolute freedom, is impressively described by Hobbes in the following passage of *Leviathan*:

It is a real unity of them all [...] as if every man should say to every man: 'I authorize and give up my right of governing myself to this man, or to this assembly of men, on this condition, that thou give up thy right to him, and authorize all his actions in like manner. This done, the multitude so united in one person is called a 'commonwealth' [...].[44]

Provided, then, that each individual agrees to forgo his "natural right to everything" and his arbitrary exercise of power it is possible for human beings to establish an "artful" state which holds their wolf-like nature in check and establishes a condition of peace. Hobbes writes in a language of high enthusiasm about this solemn transfer of the power of all individuals to the "commonwealth":

This is the generation of that great *Leviathan* [...], of that Mortal God to which we owe [...] our peace and defence.[45]

Here, the "war of all against all" is replaced by an ordered social coexistence. The agreement to collectively forgo the "natural right to everything" is, considered purely pragmatically, a very rational and sensible one. But when one looks closely at Hobbes's most fundamental assumptions regarding human nature the question necessarily arises of whether these assumptions involve an internal contradiction. Why, in fact, would beings whose nature is essentially wolfish and power-oriented all of a sudden behave so sensibly and rationally as to agree collectively to give up their individual powers? Hobbes poses this question himself and answers it as follows:

The final cause, end or design of men, who naturally love liberty and dominion over others in the introduction of that restraint upon themselves in which we see them

live in commonwealths is the foresight of their own preservation [...], that is to say, of getting themselves out of that miserable condition of war.[46]

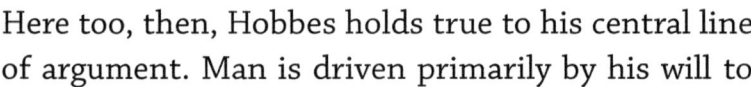

Here too, then, Hobbes holds true to his central line of argument. Man is driven primarily by his will to self-preservation and to power, so that even the contract to forgo this power and to establish a state are not really acts of reason but rather arise from this very will to self-preservation. More specifically, they arise from the fear of death:

> The passions that incline men to peace are fear of death (and) desire of such things as are necessary to commodious living [...] And reason suggesteth convenient articles of peace upon which men may be drawn to agreement.[47]

Also worthy of note in Hobbes's remarks about the agreement that founds a stable and peaceful society is his use of the phrase "as if...":

> It is a real unity of them all [...] as if every man should say to every man: 'I authorize and give up my right of governing myself [...] on this condition, that thou give up thy right (to do so as well).[48]

By his use of the hypothetical "as if" here, Hobbes gives us to understand that the agreement in question was perhaps never formulated or concluded in just this way and may indeed never be so even at any point in humanity's future. This possibility of its unreality persists even though such a primordial agreement or contract would be the sole logical legitimation for the legitimacy of state power. Scholars of Hobbes's work have spoken, therefore, of a "hypothetical contract". And indeed even Hobbes himself concedes that there never actually existed, generally across the entire world, any such "state of Nature", nor any such contractual exit from it, as he describes:

It may peradventure be thought (that) there was never such a time nor condition of war as this. And I believe that it was never generally so over all the world. But there are many places where they live so now.[49]

Hobbes does indeed point out, at this point in the text of his principal work, that in certain uncivilized regions of the world people still lived, in Hobbes's own day, as if "everyone had a right to everything" and that in such regions certain Indian tribes, for example, existed in a "state of Nature", constantly making war on one another. But it is not, in the end, with such real historical circumstances that Hobbes is concerned. His concern is rather the logical consistency of his argument about the basis of the state's legitimacy. Human beings leave the "state of Nature", he argues, by coming to a contractual agreement that all shall give up, thenceforth, their "natural right to everything". That is to say, they shall forgo, in future, such practices as lynching and taking justice into their own hands as they may have engaged in previously and, no longer ruthlessly pursuing their own interests, shall abide by the laws established by the ruling state authority.

It follows logically, then, that the main task of this ruling state authority, and the only justification for its existence, consists in its establishing and securing a peaceful coexistence on the basis of which every citizen can pursue his own interests and realize his own notion of personal happiness. This argument, or political design, sketched out by Hobbes as long ago as 1651 contains, in essence, all the key elements of our modern notion of a state characterized by the rule of law and based on free-market principles: i.e. a state which allows its citizens to freely develop their individual personalities within a certain fixed set of legal rules.

The State as Guarantor of Human Coexistence

It is the state alone, with its complete monopoly on power, which can ensure that human beings will live peacefully with one another and that the country of their habitations shall flourish. This central thesis of Hobbes's is given graphic expression in the still-fascinating image that he chose as the frontispiece for the first, English edition of his *Leviathan*, published in 1651.

Here, one sees the figure of the sovereign, with a sword in his right hand and a bishop's crook in his left. This symbolizes that, in Hobbes's vision, the sovereign authority would combine both state and ecclesiastical power. Nowhere in the image is any general, nobleman or high church dignitary to be seen. Because, in the world that Hobbes envisages, no one else has at his disposal any power that can even distantly compare to that of the sovereign. At the uppermost edge of the image, above the crown, there can be read the inscription:

Non est potestas super terram quae comparetur ei (No power on earth can be compared to his).[50]

This, for Hobbes, is a crucially important point. Because as soon as individual citizens or groups of citizens, such as Mafiosi, religious fanatics, or parties to some political civil war, begin themselves to exert power, and perhaps even to acquire more influence than the sovereign, this latter is no longer in a position to guarantee compliance with the law and thus the safety and security of the other citizens. Where such a situation arises, the citizens must return to the practice of defending and protecting themselves and are thereby no longer bound to respect the contract by which the state was founded:

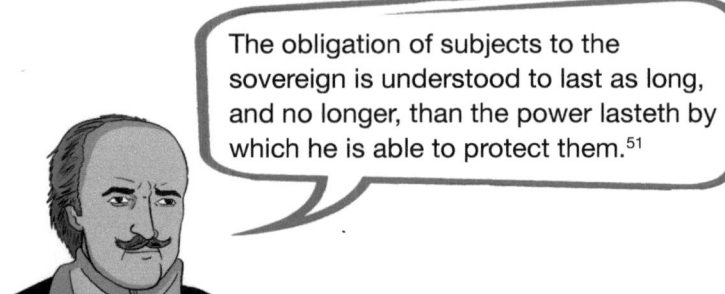

> The obligation of subjects to the sovereign is understood to last as long, and no longer, than the power lasteth by which he is able to protect them.[51]

If the sovereign, then, is to protect his subjects permanently and effectively, he needs an absolute monopoly on power. This is why Hobbes chose a frontispiece for his book in which the sovereign is represented as a gigantic human figure that towers above and dwarfs all the fields, mountains and cities of the landscape that surrounds him. On a superficial glance the figure representing the sovereign appears to be wearing some sort of chain-mail vest to protect him against attacks. But when one looks closer one sees that the little shapes that form his torso are not at all the links in a chain-mail vest but rather countless little human figures who are all turned attentively in the direction of the sovereign's head.

By specifying this detail of the frontispiece, Hobbes doubtless wished to convey the idea that the body of the state is formed by the citizens themselves, who do so by contracting together and thus creating, collectively, the ruling power. It is also significant, however, that the tight mass of citizens does not extend above the torso and form the sovereign's head as well. The head remains free, and that of a single being, because the ruler, once he has been established and installed as such, is to stand above the interests of all citizens and groups of citizens and pass just laws independently of all possible influence by those he rules.

For all that, though, the image unmistakably expresses an asymmetry between the ruler and the ruled, showing the citizens to all be oriented to the centre of power without this latter reciprocating this orientation. And indeed Hobbes does give a very one-sided account of the sovereign's rights in contrast to those of his subjects:

> And if this sovereignty be truly and indeed transferred, the state or commonwealth is an absolute monarchy wherein the monarch

> is at liberty to dispose as well of the succession as of the possession, and not an elective kingdom.[52]

Likewise in law-making the sovereign is to enjoy a completely free hand:

> [...] The commonwealth alone prescribes and commands the observation of those rules which we call law [...] But the commonwealth (has no) capacity

> to do anything except through [...] the sovereign; and therefore the sovereign is the sole legislator [...] None can abrogate a law (already) made but the sovereign.[53]

Citizens can neither abrogate nor alter laws. They have no influence on law-making. The sovereign, however, remains absolutely free:

The sovereign of a commonwealth [...] is not subject to the civil laws.[54]

Since Hobbes was writing in an era of progress and enlightenment, already some of his own contemporaries raised criticisms of this total subjection, in Hobbes's model of the state, of the people to the sovereign power. Many took especial exception to the idea that this power could not be removed even if its practice of government proved poor or odious. Hobbes himself acknowledges such objections but repudiates them on the grounds that we have already examined:

And though of so unlimited a power men may fancy many evil consequences, yet the consequences of the want of it, which is perpetual

war of every man against his neighbour, are much worse.[55]

Of What Use Is Hobbes's Discovery For Us Today?

Not Our Nature But Rather the Taming of Our Nature Makes Survival Possible. Is Hobbes Right?

Of what use is Hobbes to us today? The picture he draws of an absolutist state is not an attractive one for us. Indeed, for many it appears to be something so unappealing as to be beneath serious discussion. Citizens in Hobbes's imagined state have no way of protecting themselves against the excesses of state power. The sovereign's time in office is not limited, nor is there any way to vote him out. The state that Hobbes envisages likewise lacks anything resembling an independent judiciary or a Supreme Court at which complaint might be lodged against infractions of the constitution by the sovereign power. There can be little doubt that, impelled by his overriding anxiety that the state might lose the authority that it needs to keep the peace, Hobbes accorded too much power to the sovereign. Comparing this sovereign to the sea-monster Leviathan in the Bible, he made of him a monster indeed. From the perspective of most readers today, then, Hobbes will appear to have offered a solution as bad or worse than the problem he set out to solve.

But can we say, at least, that the terms he posed the problem in were valid ones? Is it really the case, as Hobbes supposed, that in the absence of laws, norms and institutions human beings become grave risks to one another's survival? Do we really need the state in order to organize our coexistence and protect us from one another? And do we really fall back inevitably into the "state of Nature" and "the war of all against all" if the state begins to lose its authority over us?

These questions are difficult to answer if one attempts to do so simply by reference to the empirical facts. Hobbes himself, indeed, offers in support of his arguments the chaotic situation that tends to arise during a civil war:

> [...] It may be perceived what manner of life there would be, where there were no common power to fear, by the manner of life that men [...] (are used) to degenerate into in a civil war.[56]

Hobbes's thought and sensibility were heavily marked by what he had seen of the terrible plundering and assault that characterized the Thirty Years War, which he had observed from afar as a young man, and the English Civil War, which he lived through in his later years:

> For the root [...] of all misfortune is war, principally civil war. From it spring murder, devastation and dearth of all things.[57]

There are doubtless to be found in history many other examples of dark epochs in which there was no state authority to keep the peace, no "Leviathan" to hold Man's wolf-like nature in check. Thus, far from their homes, medieval crusaders were able to burn whole cities to the ground and, in more recent times, soldiers were able to use the chaos of the world wars to plunder and to rape. Such cases, indeed, may have been exceptions; or at least it may have been only a minority of medieval warriors or modern citizen soldiers who seized this opportunity to do such things. But the fact remains that places ungoverned by law in which no punishment needs to be expected do indeed encourage theft, robbery and abuse. Hobbes formulates this in a still more radical way:

[...] Justice and equity of themselves, without the terror of some power to cause them to be observed, are contrary to our natural passions.[58]

How little restraint human beings tend to show by themselves once the external restraining power is removed can be seen from the police-documented accounts of the events that occurred in New York in the great "black-out" of 1977.

On the 13th of July of that year, at 9.36 pm, the lights went out all over the huge city. Nor, for a whole 25 hours, did the city's traffic-lights, air-conditioners, elevators, subway trains or hospitals have any power. Nine million people were plunged into darkness. The consequences of this bear a disturbing resemblance to Hobbes's vision of Man in a "state of Nature".

Marauding hordes of thieves, some habitual and some merely taking one-time advantage of the situation, plundered more than 1600 shops and stores and set more than a thousand fires.

In the course of the night some ten thousand people went roaming through the darkened streets, looting. An orgy of violence gripped the entire city. The mayor declared a state of emergency and mobilized all the resources of the peace-keeping authority (or, if one will, the "Leviathan") to try to ensure the safety of citizens. Eight thousand policemen were sent out into the burning streets and made a total of 3,776 arrests. The prisons, however, were very soon full beyond capacity and many others remained un-arrested. Some 463 of these policemen were injured, many seriously, and two people died in that night's many fires. Finally, New York's police force proved completely overtaxed by the situation and could only stand back and watch as the city descended into chaos. A journalist described what happened next: "'It's Christmas!', the looters were shouting. They came rushing up to the stores with trolleys and even small trucks. Husbands, mothers, and teenage boys and girls grabbed and ran off with all that was not nailed to the floor, be it TVs, refrigerators, electric ovens, food, nappies, jewellery, alcohol, furniture or drugs.

Even children joined in the frenzy of theft and robbery. Store-owners were forced to arm themselves with pistols, rifles and baseball bats just in order to preserve their livelihoods. In the Bronx some fifty cars were stolen, with a total value of 250,000 dollars. Not far from there, a furniture store lost goods worth 55,000 dollars. In Bedford-Stuyvesant police arrested a man running away with three hundred kitchen-sink plugs. Many looters and robbers were robbed by others before they could carry their booty home. 'This is a night of wild beasts', said one policeman."[59]

These descriptions do indeed uncannily recall Hobbes's description of the "state of Nature":

Where there is no common power, there is no law; and where there is no law, no injustice [...] It is consequent also to the same condition that there be no property [...] but only that to be every man's that he can get, and for so long as he can keep it.[60]

In New York, indeed, struggles broke out not just between individuals but also between groups over the potential booty. Each one tried to wrest what had been plundered from the hands of other plunderers. Once the marauding bands reached the neighbourhood of Little Italy, the Mafiosi who still, at the time, controlled this quarter of the city joined together to seal their territory off and beat back the mob. Armed self-defence of the sort engaged in by these local gangsters, and also by store-owners defending their stores with guns and baseball bats, is something which, on Hobbes's terms, is entirely understandable and legitimate under conditions in which the state power can no longer ensure safety and security:

[...] If there be no power erected, or not great enough for our security, every man will, and may lawfully, rely on his own strength and art for caution against other men.[61]

One is tempted indeed, in view of what occurred in New York, to concur entirely in Hobbes's arguments about a "war of all against all" and an essentially "wolf-like" nature of Man which breaks out as soon as restraining power is removed. It might, however, be objected to any such unconditional agreement with Hobbes that, although tens of thousands did engage in looting and plundering, the majority of New York's nine million inhabitants continued to live peacefully even under these conditions, i.e. revealed no "wolf-like" nature after all. Furthermore, the scenes we have described did not occur everywhere in the city but principally in underprivileged areas like the Bronx.

Hobbes, however, would surely see this latter detail rather as confirmation of his philosophy, which specifies "the struggle for scarce commodities" as one of the three main causes of conflict in the state of Nature. On these terms, it does indeed seem logically consistent that such conflict should break out first where goods and commodities are most scarce. Moreover, Hobbes would surely also have made the argument that, had the state not been able to re-establish control on the very next day after the blackout, the inhabitants also of the city's less underprivileged areas would have armed themselves and seen to their own safety.

The "Lord of the Flies" Scenario: Without a State, Do We Fall Back Into Barbarism?

Hobbes's warning that a fall back into a "state of Nature" is possible at any time has been a theme taken up not just by philosophers but also by authors of great literature. Three hundred years after the writing of *Leviathan* the Nobel-Prize-winning British novelist William Golding achieved worldwide success with his novel *Lord of the Flies*.

It tells the story of some British boarding-school pupils who, surviving a plane-crash, land up on an isolated tropical island. There, far away from all civilization, they find themselves in a state much like Hobbes's "state of Nature".

No adults have survived the crash but, raised in the stratified world of the British class system, the boys naturally choose a chief, who is to lead the group and settle any differences that may arise among them. But in the solitude and wilderness of their new home that truth is borne out that is so succinctly enunciated by Hobbes:

Justice and injustice [...] are qualities that relate to man in society, not in solitude.[62]

Despite being "well-brought-up boys", then, the pupils swiftly lose, there on their lonely island, all sense of right and wrong. The boy chosen to lead the group, Ralph, is of a character, indeed, well suited to this leadership role, which he carries out, at first, with skill and intelligent circumspection. But his rival, Jack, takes the boys' election of Ralph as a personal insult and broods on ways of taking his revenge.

The division of labour decided upon is such that Jack, along with some chosen helpers, provides the community with food by hunting wild boar. In this way he is able to establish a power-position of his own as "king of the hunters", while the other boys carry out such apparently less important functions as maintaining the signal fire and constructing shelters. Finally, however, Jack feels confident enough to declare himself the true leader of the group, sparking off a bitter struggle over power and honour. In the course of this struggle the boys take to painting their faces with war-paint and descend further and further into savagery, which leads eventually to not just one but two murders.

Driven by fear, more and more of the boys take the side of the armed and violent Jack until Ralph is left as sole surviving member of the opposite camp. "He argued unconvincingly that they would let him alone, perhaps even make an outlaw of him".[63] But then he realizes the bitter truth: "These painted savages would go further and further".[64]

And indeed Jack and his hunters eventually track Ralph down and drive him onto the beach where, just when they are about to kill him, a ship of the British navy finally arrives and rescues the boys. The officer who disembarks from it is shocked to see the war-paint and to learn of the murders. Horrified, he upbraids the well-brought-up boarding-school boys with the words: "I should have thought that a pack of British boys – you're all British, aren't you? – would have been able to put up a better show than that."[65]

Golding's novel is, indeed, only a work of fiction. But it shows, nonetheless, in a very impressive manner how quickly human beings leave civilization behind them. The German literary critic Karl Korn has very rightly observed that "Poetry and bitter truth have seldom been so close to being one and the same as in this book".[66]

The Stanford Prison Experiment: How Do We Handle Power When Nothing is Forbidden?

Although Golding's novel is fiction, the so-called "Stanford Prison Experiment" of 1971 allows us a real-life insight into the behaviour of people who, for a limited period of time, have all force of moral coercion removed from them and are able to take their decisions in a space free of all laws and regulations. The results of this experiment are quite as disturbing as the world evoked in Golding's novel.

The American psychologists Philip Zimbardo, Craig Haney and Curtis Banks recruited, at Stanford University, 24 middle-class students with a view to investigating human behaviour under prison conditions. Half of the students were assigned to take over, for a period of two weeks, the role of "guards" and were issued with uniforms, sun-glasses and rubber truncheons; the other half were assigned the role of "prisoners" and, after delousing, were issued hospital nightgowns with numbers sewn into them, nylon stockings drawn over their hair and heavy chains on their feet. As the "prison" there functioned a specially-adapted cellar of the university building.

It was the task of the "guards" to prevent escapes and to keep order within the "prison". In order to do this, they were allowed the freedom to establish their own rules and to take all measures which they deemed necessary to this end.

Whereas, at the start, the participants in the experiment tried out their assigned roles, and the possibilities these roles offered, only in a cautious and tentative manner, already on the second day the situation began to escalate. The "guards" began to prevent those "prisoners" who had displayed any sort of resistance from using the toilets situated in the corridor and to force them to defecate in buckets in their cells. They punished them by spraying them with cold carbon dioxide from fire extinguishers that they had found in the cellar of the university. If a "prisoner" did so much as smile during rollcall he was shouted at, forced to explain himself and severely punished. These over-reactions on the part of the "guards" occurred in response not just to real but even to purely imagined signs of disrespect on the part of the "prisoners". They were, in other words, examples of what Hobbes calls

"[...] Quarrels arising from (a concern with) glory [...]"[67]

which can be triggered by

"(Such) trifles as a word, a smile [...] or any other sign of undervalue."[68]

From the third day onward the "guards" began to humiliate the "prisoners" by taking their clothes away and severely punished any protest or critique. One participant was already too stressed to continue and left the experiment. And indeed from this point on the scientific supervisor Zimbardo found himself having to intervene more and more often, in his role as "Chief Warden", to prevent real acts of physical mistreatment. But even this did not stop further "prisoners" from suffering emotional breakdowns and having to be removed from the experiment. On the sixth day the "guards" began to inflict such cruel and extensive physical punishments on the "prisoners" that the experiment had to be broken off. It had been noted that especially during the night, when the cameras became unable to record clear images, the "guards" began to torment and bully the "prisoners" in the most inhuman ways.

There has, indeed, been much scientific criticism of the protocols adopted in the Stanford Prison Experiment. It has been objected, for example, that the organizer of the experiment, Zimbardo, ought not at the same time to have played a role within it (that of "Chief Warden"). It has also been suggested that the students recruited for the experiment were often not displaying spontaneous behaviour of their own but rather acting out roles that they had absorbed, for example, from films that they had seen about prison life.

The fact remains, however, that the terrible mistreatments that made it necessary to break off the experiment before it had run its full course represent at least a strong indication that human beings have great difficulty handling power when it is given to them, as it was to the "guards" in the Stanford study, with no defined limits set:

For every man looketh that his companion should value him at the same rate as he sets upon himself; and, upon all signs of contempt or undervaluing, naturally endeavours to extort a greater value from his contemnors, by damage, and from others, by the example.[69]

The Inner and the Outer Leviathan in Hobbes and Freud

Hobbes's theory also receives much support from psychoanalysis. Above all from its founder, Sigmund Freud. Freud emphatically confirms Hobbes's vision of Man's nature and even cites Hobbes verbatim: "The element of truth behind all this is [...] that men are not gentle creatures who want to be loved and who can, at the most, defend themselves when they are attacked. They are, on the contrary, creatures among whose instinctual endowments is to be reckoned a powerful share of aggressiveness. As a result, their neighbour is for them not only a potential helper or sexual object but also someone who tempts them to satisfy their aggressiveness on him, to exploit his capacity for work without compensation, to use him sexually without his consent, to seize his possessions, to humiliate him, to cause him pain, to torture and to kill him. *Homo homini lupus est*: who, in the face of all his experience of life and history, will have the courage to dispute this assertion? [...] Civilization has to use its utmost resources in order to set limits to Man's aggressive instincts [...]"[70]

It is clear from this passage that Freud shares that core idea of Hobbes whereby it is not Man's natural drives that secure our coexistence but rather, on the contrary, culture that must "use its utmost resources" in order to keep these drives in check. Freud, however, adds to Hobbes's social theory one further important element: the so-called "inner Leviathan". Because, Freud argues, what ensures compliance with the imperatives of culture is not just that "outer Leviathan" represented by the state along with its laws and its police forces but also and above all a kind of "inner Leviathan" in the form of our conscience.

Moreover, this conscience or, as Freud calls it, the "super-ego", keeps us, with its scruples and impulses to self-punishment, under quite as strict and harsh a surveillance as does the state. There are gathered in the super-ego, says Freud, all the moral values, rules, convictions and taboos which we have acquired and learned since earliest childhood. The super-ego, then, functions as a sort of internal place-holder for the external Leviathan. We internalize the external coercions and the super-ego takes on the role of the censor. If we had not, for example, already stored away in our super-ego the command "thou shalt not steal" or the belief that "property must be respected", the number of shoplifting cases would be much higher than it is. The external Leviathan, even with all its store detectives and policemen, could never prevent all these potential criminal acts if it were not being lent a constant tacit support by the internal self-restrictions of the super-ego.

Freud, then, adds a decisive supplement to Hobbes's basic design. Like Hobbes, he believes that the coercions and impositions of culture are, at bottom, necessary. Freud, however, is critical of the excesses of both the outer and the inner Leviathan in a way that Hobbes is not. In his famous book *Civilization and Its*

Discontents Freud argues that, although bans and taboos are certainly needed, culture often imposes on us more interdictions than are necessary and than, indeed, are healthy. There exists a danger, he points out, that people who are obliged to respect too many cultural restrictions may fall victim to neuroses.

Freud, then, looked more sceptically on the state and on cultural taboos than did Hobbes. It is interesting, however, that this experienced psychoanalyst, who was in daily contact with patients and drew what knowledge he had from direct therapeutic experience, came finally to the same philosophical conclusion as Hobbes: it is not our basic instincts that ensure that we can live together as social beings but rather the taming of these instincts by civilization. Thus, Freud writes: "The existence of this inclination to aggression, which we can detect in ourselves and justly assume to be present in others, is the factor which disturbs our relations with our neighbour and which forces civilization into such a high expenditure of energy."[71]

Timeless Hobbes

Hobbes was born in 1588, 90 years after the discovery of America. He is, therefore, a man of the early modern period. With his revolutionary ideas, however, he took a radical stance against the notions dominant in the Middle Ages. He was the first philosopher to dare to contradict the religious belief in the originally peaceful nature of the first human beings, Adam and Eve, living innocently in Paradise. Human beings are not, argued Hobbes, beings created in the image of God, as the Bible claims, who lost their place in Paradise only due to a Satanic temptation and will return there in the afterlife.

We modern human beings, Hobbes insisted, must look reality in the face. And this means: understand that we do not, by nature, tend toward an Eden-like goodness, altruism and love of our neighbours but rather toward self-preservation and the maximization of our own personal advantage. It is only when we are honest with ourselves about this fact that we can draw the necessary conclusions for our social co-existence.

In contrast to the notion of the "divine right of kings", whereby the ruling monarch is directly chosen by God, on Hobbes's account of things human beings have the task of organizing their own governments. And in the place of Aristotle's vision of Man as an essentially and fundamentally social being Hobbes advances for the first time a theory of the human being as a bourgeois "individual" in the radical sense, whose personal interests must always be taken into account.

These positively seditious ideas were far too radical for many of Hobbes's contemporaries. Three years after his death his work was declared blasphemous and heretical and placed under a ban. The professors and students of the University of Oxford solemnly burned all his books. But they did so in vain. The key new ideas he had introduced into philosophical discourse could not be extinguished.

His warning image of the wolf-like nature of Man became graven, in subsequent centuries, deeply into people's collective memory. It is not by chance that we still quote Hobbes so often today.

But of what use are Hobbes's ideas to us really? Does his pessimism serve some useful purpose or can its negativity lead, in the end, only to frustration? It is easy to harbour a deep ambivalence about Hobbes in this regard. This is the way, for example, that one of his greatest critics, Jean-Jacques Rousseau, felt about Hobbes's work, which at the same time attracted and repelled him. In one of his major works, The Social Contract, Rousseau writes of Hobbes: "What made his political theory obnoxious was not the fact that some of it was false and abhorrent but rather that some was right and true."[72]

Hobbes's deeply pessimistic philosophy of human nature remains provocative still today. The age-old philosophical question of whether Man is, as Aristotle, Hegel and Marx contended, an essentially social and sociable being and therefore by nature "good" or whether, as was argued by Hobbes, Nietzsche and Adam Smith, Man is by nature an individualist guided by self-interest alone is clearly a question too ramified to try to settle here. What is most decisive, however, is not Hobbes's philosophy of Man so much as the conclusions he drew from it.

On the one hand he urges us to be cautious, since in the absence of a state to keep order we can slip back at any time into a barbaric condition. For Hobbes nothing separates us from our "wolf-like nature" except a tenuous layer formed by the laws. The great historian Hans Mommsen speaks in this connection of a "thin patina of civilization" which we can shatter and lose at any moment. The word "patina" is derived from Latin and means "thin membrane". How thin this membrane of civilization remains even in our own modern societies is shown, for example, by the "ethnic cleansings" that recently occurred in the very heart of Europe during the break-up of Yugoslavia.

On the other hand, Hobbes issues the equally timeless reminder that we should look upon the state as an artificial entity that we ourselves create for our own protection. This simple notion was revolutionary in Hobbes's age and remains so today. Indeed, with his three-part logic of argumentation, deploying the notions "state of Nature", "contract" and "state", Hobbes founds modern political theory and the modern understanding of democracy pretty much in their entirety.

"We, the people, are the state" runs the credo which sums up, still in our present age, the self-understanding of democrats. Nowhere is this credo more plainly and graphically illustrated than in the frontispiece of Hobbes's *Leviathan*. The state consists of nothing else but we ourselves, its many citizens. We create it by giving up our "natural right to everything" in favour of a sovereign individual or assembly who will then, henceforth, bear the sword of political authority in his or their hands alone and will alone see to it that order and peace are maintained.

In Hobbes's version, indeed, this sovereign is accorded dictatorial, almost absolute power and need make, in return, no commitment to the people he wields power over beyond the minimal one of preserving their physical safety. But even, indeed above all, for Hobbes the central idea here is that the sovereign's power is derived solely and exclusively from the contract entered into by the people. And from this idea it was just a small step to the demand raised later by the men and women of the French Revolution: "Who is to rule the people if not the people themselves?"

Rousseau, then, was only being logically consistent in supplementing Hobbes's model of the state with a demand for direct rule by the people. So too was Montesquieu in building upon Hobbes's vision a vision of "division of powers" into executive, legislative and judiciary. Because for Montesquieu it is absolutely necessary that the sovereign, be he king or elected government, be limited in his or their powers. The government can and should rule the people through its ministers and civil servants; but it should not have the power to make laws independently of parliament and must itself remain subject to the judgments of politically impartial judges.

For all that, though, Hobbes remains the true pioneer among modern theorists of the state. Because it was

Hobbes who first threw into the ring the challenging contention that political rule can only be legitimate if it serves the interests of citizens and arises from a free decision by these latter to commit themselves to obeying it. This is so insofar as, as Hobbes saw, each one of us is naturally and irreducibly his own master and has to decide his own fate. It is in Hobbes's philosophy, then, that that "free individual" who stands at the centre of our modern age and experience is born.

Bibliographical References

1   Thomas Hobbes, Leviathan, With Selected Variants from the Latin Edition of 1668, edited by E. Curley, Hackett Publishing, Indianapolis and Cambridge, p. 77, note 7.

2   Thomas Hobbes, De Cive, The English Version, Volume 3 of the Clarendon Edition of the Philosophical Works of Thomas Hobbes, Clarendon Press, Oxford, 1983, p. 24

3   Thomas Hobbes, Leviathan, Oxford World's Classics edition, Oxford University Press, Oxford, 1996, p. 447

4   Ibid.

5   Thomas Hobbes, De Cive, The English Version, Volume 3 of the Clarendon Edition of the Philosophical Works of Thomas Hobbes, Clarendon Press, Oxford, 1983, p. 32

6   Ibid. p. 34.

7   Ibid.

8   Thomas Hobbes De Homine in Hobbes, Man and Citizen, translated by Charles T. Wood, Hackett Publishing, Indianapolis and Cambridge, 1991, p. 48.

9   Thomas Hobbes, Leviathan, Oxford World's Classics edition, Oxford University Press, Oxford, 1996, p. 66.

10   Ibid.

11   Thomas Hobbes, De Cive, The English Version, Volume 3 of the Clarendon Edition of the Philosophical Works of Thomas Hobbes, Clarendon Press, Oxford, 1983, p. 34.

12   Ibid. p. 49.

13   Thomas Hobbes, Leviathan, Oxford World's Classics edition, Oxford University Press, Oxford, 1996, p. 7.

14   In the 2nd-century-BC comedy "Asinaria" we find the phrase in the slightly longer form lupus est homo homini, non homo. The phrase would doubtless have long since been completely forgotten if Hobbes had not made it famous through his Leviathan.

15   Thomas Hobbes, Leviathan, Oxford World's Classics edition, Oxford University Press, Oxford, 1996, p. 83.

16   Ibid. p. 85.

17   Ibid. p. 84.

18 Ibid. p. 85.
19 Ibid. p. 83
20 Ibid.
21 Thomas Hobbes De Homine in Hobbes, Man and Citizen, translated by Charles T. Wood, Hackett Publishing, Indianapolis and Cambridge, 1991, p. 40
22 Thomas Hobbes, Leviathan, Oxford World's Classics edition, Oxford University Press, Oxford, 1996, p. 66.
23 Ibid. p. 83.
24 Ibid. pp. 83-84.
25 Ibid. p. 82.
26 Ibid. p. 82.
27 Ibid. p. 83.
28 Ibid. p. 84.
29 Ibid. p. 83.
30 Ibid. p. 84.
31 Ibid.
32 Aristotle, Politics, translated by Benjamin Jowett, Clarendon Press, Oxford, 1885, p. 4
33 Thomas Hobbes, Leviathan, Oxford World's Classics edition, Oxford University Press, Oxford, 1996, p. 113.
34 Ibid.
35 Ibid.
36 Ibid.
37 Ibid. p. 7.
38 Thomas Hobbes, De Cive, The English Version, Volume 3 of the Clarendon Edition of the Philosophical Works of Thomas Hobbes, Clarendon Press, Oxford, 1983, pp 47-48.
39 Thomas Hobbes, Leviathan, Oxford World's Classics edition, Oxford University Press, Oxford, 1996, p. 87.
40 Ibid.
41 Ibid. p. 106.
42 Ibid. p. 111.
43 Ibid.
44 Ibid. p. 114.
45 Ibid.
46 Ibid. p. 111.
47 Ibid. p. 86.

48 Ibid. p. 114.

49 Ibid. p. 85.

50 Ibid. Frontispiece. At the end of this Latin sentence its source too is noted: the Biblical "Book of Job", Chapter 41, Verse 24. The verse in question describes the terrific sea-monster Leviathan which Hobbes chose as a symbol for his ideal state because the Biblical writer states that "there is not his like upon the earth" and he exerts power over all through the fear that he inspires.

51 Ibid. p. 147.

52 Thomas Hobbes, Human Nature and De Corpore Politico, edited by J.C.A Gaskin, Oxford University Press, 1994, p. 121.

53 Thomas Hobbes, Leviathan, Oxford World's Classics edition, Oxford University Press, Oxford, 1996, p. 176.

54 Ibid.

55 Ibid. p. 138.

56 Ibid. p. 85.

57 Thomas Hobbes, Human Nature and De Corpore Politico, edited by J.C.A Gaskin, Oxford University Press, 1994, p. 22

58 Thomas Hobbes, Leviathan, Oxford World's Classics edition, Oxford University Press, Oxford, 1996, p. 111.

59 Taken from the article Blackout of 1977 : New York's Darkest Night by Mark Pitzke, published in Der Spiegel Online, 13.07.2007.

60 Thomas Hobbes, Leviathan, Oxford World's Classics edition, Oxford University Press, Oxford, 1996, p. 85.

61 Ibid. p. 111.

62 Ibid. p. 85

63 William Golding, Lord of the Flies, Penguin Great Books of the Twentieth Century, Penguin, New York, 2000, p. 166

64 Ibid.

65 Ibid. p. 182.

66 Karl Korn in the Frankfurter Allgemeine Zeitung.

67 Thomas Hobbes, Leviathan, Oxford World's Classics edition, Oxford University Press, Oxford, 1996, pp. 83-4

68 Ibid.

69 Ibid.

70 Sigmund Freud, Civilization and Its Discontents, translated by James Strachey, W.W. Norton and Company, New York, 1962, pp. 58-59

71   Ibid. p. 59
72   Jean-Jacques Rousseau, Discourse on Political Economy and The Social Contract, Oxford University Press 1994, p. 161.

Already published in the same series:

Walther Ziegler
Camus in 60 Minutes
ISBN 9783741227738

Walther Ziegler
Freud in 60 Minutes
ISBN 9783741227707

Walther Ziegler
Hegel in 60 Minutes
ISBN 9783741227677

Walther Ziegler
Heidegger in 60 Minutes
ISBN 9783741227752

Walther Ziegler
Kant in 60 Minutes
ISBN 9783741226373

Walther Ziegler
Marx in 60 Minutes
ISBN 9783741227691

Walther Ziegler
Nietzsche in 60 Minutes
ISBN 9783752803822

Walther Ziegler
Platon in 60 Minutes
ISBN 9783741227615

Walther Ziegler
Sartre in 60 Minutes
ISBN 9783741227653

Walther Ziegler
Rousseau in 60 Minutes
ISBN 9783741227622

Walther Ziegler
Smith in 60 Minutes
ISBN 9783741227721

Walther Ziegler
Rawls in 60 Minutes
ISBN 9783750424050

Walther Ziegler
Wittgenstein in 60 Minutes

Walther Ziegler
Adorno in 60 Minutes

Walther Ziegler
Hobbes in 60 Minutes

Walther Ziegler
Popper in 60 Minutes

Coming soon in the same series:

Walther Ziegler
Arendt in 60 Minutes

Walther Ziegler
Foucault in 60 Minutes

Walther Ziegler
Habermas in 60 Minutes

Walther Ziegler
Schopenhauer in 60 Minutes

The author:

Dr Walther Ziegler is academically trained in the fields of philosophy, history and political science. As a foreign correspondent, reporter and newsroom coordinator for the German TV station ProSieben he has produced films on every continent. His news reports have won several prizes and awards. He has also authored numerous books in the field of philosophy. His many years of experience as a journalist mean that he is able to present the complex ideas of the great philosophers in a way that is both engaging and very clear. Since 2007 he has also been active as a teacher and trainer of young TV journalists in Munich, holding the post of Academic Director at the Media Academy, a University of Applied Sciences that offers film and TV courses at its base directly on the site of the major European film production company Bavaria Film. After the huge success of the book series "Great thinkers in 60 Minutes", he works as a freelance writer and philosopher.